LET'S LEARN VERBS!

RUN!

BY KATE MIKOLEY

Gareth Stevens
PUBLISHING

Please visit our website, www.garethstevens.com. For a free color catalog of all our high-quality books, call toll free 1-800-542-2595 or fax 1-877-542-2596.

Cataloging-in-Publication Data

Names: Mikoley, Kate.
Title: Let's learn verbs! / Kate Mikoley.
Description: New York : Gareth Stevens Publishing, 2019. | Series: Wonderful world of words | Includes glossary and index.
Identifiers: LCCN ISBN 9781538218976 (pbk.) | ISBN 9781538218952 (library bound) | ISBN 9781538218983 (6 pack)
Subjects: LCSH: English language–Verb–Juvenile literature. | English language–Parts of speech–Juvenile literature.
Classification: LCC PE1355.M57 2019 | DDC 428.2'4–dc23

Published in 2019 by
Gareth Stevens Publishing
111 East 14th Street, Suite 349
New York, NY 10003

Designer: Katelyn E. Reynolds
Editor: Emily Mahoney

Photo credits: Cover, p. 1 Sergey Novikov/Shutterstock.com; p. 5 Studio 1One/ Shutterstock.com; p. 7 Alena Root/Shutterstock.com; p. 9 STUDIO GRAND OUEST/ Shutterstock.com; p. 11 CokaPoka/Shutterstock.com; p. 13 Fotokostic/Shutterstock.com; p. 15 Olesia Bilkei/Shutterstock.com; p. 17 Shahrul Azman/Shutterstock.com; p. 19 almgren /Shutterstock.com; p. 21 stockfour/Shutterstock.com.

Printed in the United States of America

CPSIA compliance information: Batch #CS18GS: For further information contact Gareth Stevens, New York, New York at 1-800-542-2595.

CONTENTS

Boldface words appear in the glossary.

Action Words

Verbs are also sometimes known as "doing" words. They **express** actions, happenings, or states of being. Words like *run*, *read*, and *smile* are all verbs. But there are many more! Be sure to check your answers to the questions in this book on page 22.

All Kinds of Actions

Some actions are physical. This means you can see with your eyes that they're happening. Verbs like *walk* and *dance* show physical actions. What verb below expresses the physical action the boy on the next page is doing?

SWIM

THINK

WATER

Other kinds of actions have to do with the things happening in your mind, called mental actions. You can't always see these actions, but they're verbs, too. *Think* is a verb that shows a mental action.

9

What's the Tense?

Verbs look and sound different **depending** on the tense. The tense is the form of the verb that shows when something happened. For example, past tense verbs show that something has already happened. These words often end with the **suffix** "-ed." What's the past tense of "cross?"

Present tense verbs show that something is happening now. If the **subject** of the sentence is "he," or "she," these verbs often have the letter "s" at the end. Which sentence below is correct?

1. He play soccer.

2. He plays soccer.

The future tense is all about things that haven't happened yet but are going to happen later. These often start with the word "will." You can say "I will sleep tonight." We know this means it's not happening yet, but it will happen.

To Be or Not to Be

The verb *be* is tricky. *Am, is, are, was,* and *were* all come from this verb. Which form is used depends on the subject and tense. Which form of "be" should you use in the following sentence if it's happening now?

Mary _____ doing her homework.

SUBJECT	Verb: *to be*		
	past tense	present tense	future tense
I	was	am	will be
YOU	were	are	will be
HE / SHE / IT	was	is	will be
WE / YOU / THEY	were	are	will be

You Use Verbs!

Verbs might seem hard to learn, but chances are you already use many of them correctly without even thinking about it. Based on the picture on the next page, what verb can you use in the following sentence?

Jamie _____ over the puddle yesterday.

There are so many verbs—and so many ways to use them! Many of the things you like to do are verbs, like playing or laughing! Verbs are one of the things that make learning about language so interesting.

GLOSSARY

depend: to be decided by something

express: to show

subject: the person, place, or thing that does the main action of a sentence

suffix: a letter or a group of letters that is added to the end of a word to change its meaning

ANSWER KEY

p. 6: swim

p. 10: crossed

p. 12: 2

p. 16: is

p. 18: jumped

FOR MORE INFORMATION

BOOKS

Blaisdell, Bette. *A Backpack Full of Verbs*. North Mankato, MN: Capstone Press, 2014.

Murray, Kara. *Verbs*. New York, NY: PowerKids Press, 2014.

Owings, Lisa. *Chase, Wiggle, Chomp: Teaching Verbs*. Mankato, MN: Child's World, 2016.

WEBSITES

Grammar Gorillas
www.funbrain.com/games/grammar-gorillas
Find the verbs and other parts of speech in this fun game.

Nouns and Verbs
www.abcya.com/nouns_and_verbs.htm
This game will help you spot verbs, while learning about nouns, too!

INDEX

5

24